Creating the life you desire
Copyright ©2022 P.B Terry-Smith

Philip B. Terry-Smith, Ph.D., Th.D., LCPC
www.drpterrysmith.com
www.coachpositive.com

ISBN: 978-0-9885429-7-6

About the Author

Dr. Philip B. Terry-Smith
Social Psychologist,
Lecturer, Teacher,
Philanthropist, Theologist,
Emergency Manager,
Humanist, Contrarian,
Humanitarian, Military Officer, Father, Husband,
Afro/Indigenous American, Musician, Gay, Motorcycle
Riding, Leather Wearing---HUMAN

 Philip B Terry-Smith is an assistant dean for Social
Sciences, Philosophy, and Interdisciplinary Studies. He
has been in academia since 1992. He has served as an
executive director and later senior director for
Emergency, International and Armed Forces Services
for the American Red Cross of the National Capital
Area and as CEO or board member for many non-profit
organizations.

He is a Colonel in the Maryland Military Department,
Maryland Defense Force. He holds a PhD in Human
Services (organizational and social systems), a non-
academic Doctor of Theology (ThD.) in comparative
spirituality, executive certificates in Law, as well as in
Social and Voluntary Sector Leadership. He maintains
a license as a professional counselor and is a certified
trauma professional and master emergency
management specialist.

Contents

You can create whatever you want. You just have to know what you want and take the opportunities as the come your way. We are who we choose to be.

~Will Smith

dedicated to my brother, J.T. Terry 1975-2021

"Chasing a person doesn't give you value or build values in you. You earn your value by chasing morality and practicing dignity."

- *SHANNON L. ALDER*

INTRODUCTION

Creating the life you want to live is perfectly within your reach! By truly embracing yourself, you're able to embrace life with excitement and gratitude. Do you need more self-compassion? How can you increase positivity in all areas of your life?

This book explores the many ways in which you can increase your feelings of self-love and self-worth and truly achieve the life you desire.

You're beyond enough. You're completely worthy of acceptance and inner peace. We will discuss these concepts in depth throughout these chapters and you'll have a stronger understanding of how to fully love yourself and live your best life.

"Doubt kills more dreams than failure ever will."

- SUZY KASSEM

CLEAR OUT ALL AREAS OF DOUBT

What are your favorite things about your life? Think for a moment about what you're grateful for. It's possible to feel that gratitude in each moment of the day. Imagine how it might feel to dive into life and pursue your true potential!

What do your days look like? What kind of people are in your life? What is your profession? What hobbies do you make time for?

You have the opportunity at any moment to take hold of your life in order to create the structure that works for you. This book is going to give you the tools that can help you begin to make changes in your life. You can develop your life however you want.

By practicing new skills and applying new concepts, you will find yourself coming out of your shell in new ways. You will love yourself in a way that makes you feel confident, worthy, and grateful. Learning about and applying self-compassion can revolutionize your lifestyle and help you live your very best life.

Shedding Your Doubt

Carrying around negativity and doubt adds a ton of weight to your shoulders. You're allowed to let go and move on from any doubt you have in your life. It's okay to be unsure and confused. That's a natural part of life.

Now you have the opportunity to begin awareness of where you have doubts. You can practice self-awareness by doing daily introspection. How do you feel when you think about work? How do you feel when you think about the relationships in your life? How do you feel about how you spend your time?

Considering these questions and paying attention to how you feel can assist in the objective observation of your daily life and inner dialogue. Your life has many components, and doubt can fester in all of them. The time has come to acknowledge those doubts and take action to be free of them.

Self-Doubt

Self-doubt is the first thing you want to let go of. If you're constantly doubting what you say or do, the time has come to make a change. If you lack confidence in any environment, it's time to transform your thinking.

Your spirit and energy can be totally drained by self-doubt. Sometimes it's difficult to realize that you're doubting yourself, especially if self-doubt has become such a natural part of your inner dialogue that you don't notice it.

Let's start by identifying how you doubt yourself, and how that doubt manifests in your life.

Questions to consider:

1. How often do you sacrifice your needs for what others want?

2. Do you frequently apologize for things you don't need to apologize for?

3. Have you ever been called or referred to yourself as a people pleaser?

4. Do you stop yourself from speaking up for yourself?

Considering these questions can help reveal any self-doubt you hold that you might not notice.

When you sacrifice your needs for others, you're putting yourself second and neglecting your own importance. When you apologize for what you don't need to, you're shaming yourself and discrediting yourself unnecessarily. You don't need to apologize for passing someone in the hallway or for asking a question.

If you find that you want everyone to like you, you might be a people pleaser. Do you go out of your way to win people over? Do you say things that contradict your values in order to gain approval of others? This is a good demonstration of self-doubt.

You're allowed to stand tall. You're allowed to speak your truth and be heard. The first step is to raise your self-awareness. Start noticing how much you value yourself compared to those around you. How does your self-doubt manifest in your behavior?

Critical Self-Talk

Self-doubt can be caused by the words you say to yourself on a daily basis. The way you see yourself and the world around you is affected by your self-talk.

When you're walking into a nerve-wracking situation, are you calming yourself in a self-compassionate way? Or are you speaking poorly to yourself about who you are and how the future will turn out?

Telling yourself that you're not enough will weigh heavily on you. Critical self-talk decreases motivation and increases unproductivity in all areas of your life.

If you don't begin to change your thinking, it will be difficult to see the many possibilities in your life. If you continue to berate yourself for the way you walk, talk, or breathe, you will only dig yourself further into a hole of negativity.

So, begin by observing your behavior and actions throughout the day. Hear your self-talk and determine whether it's positive and self-compassionate.

Negative self-talk goes hand-in-hand with self-doubt because they fuel each other. When you doubt yourself, you're not seeing yourself as worthy. When you don't believe you're worthy, you will feel self-doubt.

Doubting Relationships

Think about your community as a whole. Take an aerial view of it and see all of the connections in your life. Think about your barista at the coffee shop, your colleagues at work, your best friends, and any significant other you either have or will have in your life. Do you need more authentic connections in your life?

Begin pursuing the relationships you crave that will add meaning and purpose to your life.

Look at the connections you have with those around you. Do you feel motivated by the people close to you? Do you feel motivated by the people you work with? What's most important is the quality of your relationships.

Are there relationships in your life that you doubt? Begin by getting curious about what is underneath your doubt. How do you feel? Fearful? Resentful? Misunderstood? There are certainly things you can do to improve the quality of the relationships in your life. It's okay to crave connection. Humans are wired for that.

It's okay to doubt any relationships. You can either choose to let those relationships go with compassion, or you can decide to commit a conscious effort to make those relationships more beneficial to you.

How to Improve Personal Relationships:

1. Remain patient and compassionate. If you have a tendency to react strongly, instead, push the pause button to get back to a place of calm and compassion. Express your caring feelings by having an open mind and listening ears.

2. Actively listen. When you're having a conversation with someone close to you, be sure to give them the floor. Instead of thinking about what you want to say next, pay attention to what the person in front of you is saying. Show them that you're listening by having open body language and validating their truth.

3. Structure regular times during which you give attention to your relationships. You can go out and do an activity, make a phone call, or go get a quick coffee. The important thing is to stay in touch and reach out consistently.

4. Learn from the people closest to you. Just as those in your community can learn from you, you can learn from those in your community. Whether you're discussing your life story or learning about their line of work, there is

always something to gain from those around you.

5. Spend time around those who are positive and motivate you. If you're feeling exhausted by the relationships in your life, see what you can do to liven them up. You can also put yourself out there and meet others who will bring you to new heights.

When you're riddled with doubt, you're probably in a pretty foggy state of mind. It isn't easy to see clearly when your reality is tinted with insecurity and lack of confidence. This is how many people live their whole lives. You don't have to live this way!

Your feelings of doubt likely come from your previous years of errors, shame, and confusion. It's possible to reverse this thinking in a way that will free you from insecurity and help you focus on what is really in front of you in the moment.

Start by working on your thoughts. Do you find yourself overthinking when you're in social situations, or after you send a text message to a love-interest? It can be difficult to slow down thoughts when they feel like they're going a million miles per minute.

"Don't get too deep, it leads to over thinking, and over thinking leads to problems that doesn't even exist in the first place."

- JAYSON ENGAY

OVERTHINKING

Do you ever try to write your thoughts, but they're coming too quickly for you to write them down? Do you have that feeling of overwhelming thoughts frequently? How much time do you spend ruminating on the past?

Imagine a day where you take each moment as it comes and don't think about past moments. Imagine going to sleep at night without replaying all the wrong things you said that day. This freedom is totally possible by practicing a few new things and applying some principles to your daily life.

We all have a little nagging voice in the back of our head that can tend to narrate negative things regularly. That little nagging voice might convince you that you can tell exactly what others are thinking of you. When you believe these things, you're only creating more destruction in your own life.

Instead of replaying each conversation you've ever had, focus your attention on the present moment.

16

When we remember the past, we typically see more negative than positive.

Letting Go of The Past

What conversations or behaviors do you think about when you're replaying negativity in your head? Are there people you actively avoid because you're afraid of what they think of you?

Now is the moment where you can let yourself let go of all of those things and move forward. You no longer need to ruminate over the past. Are there memories that make you sad, angry, or fearful for the future? You can let these things go by releasing your regrets and turning them into a tool for positive growth.

How to Let Go of Regret

Follow these strategies:

1. Get curious about what, exactly, you regret. Do you regret old relationships, decisions, behaviors, or words? The regrets that cause you the most distress are important to dissolve.

2. Write about your biggest regrets. Get them apart from you so that you can look at them. Get specific about what you regret. Consider your lifestyle, behavior toward others, or decisions. Do this nonjudgmentally.

3. Look at these regrets and think about what lessons you can learn from them. Maybe you can apply one of these situations to your values. You don't need to use regrets to try to be perfect. Instead, you can look at them as opportunities to learn something new about yourself in a positive way.

4. Practice self-forgiveness. Give yourself permission to forgive yourself and grow forward. Imagine the shackles of your past dissolving. You will naturally struggle from time to time, and that's okay.

5. Decide how to move forward. Though you cannot control every aspect of life, you can

control the decisions you make based on your present moment. You don't need to hide away in shame or continue to doubt yourself. Instead, rise up and embrace each moment with a stronger of compassion for yourself.

Let your compassion for others grow. Regret helps us feel compassion for others because we can put ourselves in their shoes when sharing difficulties, even if we are on different paths. So, when you're stuck in feelings of regret, you can instantly relate to all who have felt what you feel.

You grow through both your struggles and successes. You can use these moments of regret to re-energize your efforts to live your fullest life and love yourself completely.

That Little Nagging Voice

Have you noticed any constant chatter in your head that can put a negative tint on your day? What do you do during times of frustration with yourself? You have the power to confront this voice in the back of your head that tells you that you're not enough. You can insist on the opposite, and you're right.

Start by simply hearing what you say to yourself each day, through each interaction and situation.

Think about how your motivation relates to the way you're speaking to yourself each day. When you're in a good mood, how do you talk to yourself? When you're in a bad mood and having a terrible day, observe how the way you speak to yourself changes or stays the same.

You can adjust the way you talk to yourself by replacing the negative thoughts you think with positive thoughts. It can be as simple as that. Simply come up with a thought that will oppose your critical self-talk.

For example, if you say, "I'm just going to keep disappointing people," you can replace that thought with, "I am growing each day."

This type of resetting the way you treat yourself will have a hugely positive long-term effect. You will notice your thoughts becoming more positive. Pay attention to how your mood changes as a result.

Social Anxiety

Do you overthink every social interaction you have? How do you feel when you're approaching a large group of people? Some people thrive more when they are surrounded by people. Others need some quiet time to recharge. Think about how you feel when you're in large groups.

It's common for our thoughts to speed up in social situations because we're paying attention to so many different things. The larger the crowd, the more there is to pay attention to. This can be overwhelming.

Luckily, there are simple things you can do to help ease any social anxiety you feel, regardless of the situation.

These strategies will help minimize social fear:

1. Get curious about your fear. Is there something specific that you're afraid will happen? Consider the feelings you feel

21

when you think about an upcoming social situation. What emotions arise when you're walking through a crowd or having a one-on-one coffee with someone?

2. Walk yourself through that fear by getting rational. You cannot predict the future. Bring yourself to the present moment and acknowledge that you can choose to assume this will be a good experience, or you can choose to assume it will be a negative experience.

3. Be compassionate with yourself. All moments are good times to unconditionally love yourself.

4. Ask a friend to go with you to social situations that make you nervous. You and your friend will have a stronger bond, you will do something fun together, and you will have a chance to embrace socializing with a new energy.

When you can move past this fear, you can expand your horizons even further. Continue to grow your self-compassion by moving through fear and getting curious about it, rather than shying away from anything that might be out of your comfort zone.

When you truly believe that you're worthy, you will find many of your common irrational fears drift away. As these fears dissipate, you will find yourself feeling more open and willing to have new experiences and adventures.

Getting Over Overthinking

Once you move past your negative thinking, you can begin to explore new arenas of your life. In order to best make these changes, free yourself from your negative self-talk and regret. Acknowledge the people around you and begin to open yourself up to new experiences.

When you have let go of self-doubt and begun to build your relationship with yourself, you will find that you don't ruminate negatively on your day, your past, or your future.

Your readiness to embrace the world around will give you new opportunities to thrive.

"I know there is strength in the differences between us. I know there is comfort, where we overlap."

- ANI DIFRANCO

EXPLORE YOUR COMMUNITY

Shedding self-doubt and letting go of overthinking will leave you with more motivation and confidence. When you truly appreciate yourself, fear will not hold you back in the ways that it can in times of self-loathing.

With this freedom, you can pursue activities and people that will fit into the life you want to live.

Jump In

Increase your understanding of the world around you by exploring more of it. This does not have to be taxing or time-consuming. You can start exactly where you are.

Start by observing what is around you throughout your day.

Put your phone down while you're in public places, such as the grocery store or the bookstore. You can use these moments to participate in the world around you. Look at your surroundings, at the people around you, and observe yourself in this arena. Keep your head up and try to stay open to those around you.

By showing any willingness to engage in your community, you're opening yourself up to new opportunities for connection. People are typically not as scary as we make them up to be in our heads. By attending local events and activities, you will have the opportunity to have a good time with new people while doing something you enjoy.

Consider these activities for getting involved with the world around you:

1. Be a tourist in your own town. Spend a weekend seeing the local attractions your town has to offer. Whether it's large or small, pick an adventure and go with it. You can take a walking tour, go to a museum, or

participate in a larger group activity.

2. Participate in a team sport. If you love getting active by playing your favorite sport, find a local recreational team that you can join. This will help you get to know people while doing something that you already enjoy.

3. Try something new. If you've never done a team sport, try one! If you've never been to a nice restaurant by yourself, try it! You can practice self-compassion while being kind and open to those around you.

4. Acknowledge the people you see frequently. If you have the same barista three days per week, or you see the same person at the gas station every time, acknowledge them. Though you hardly play a role in each other's 'lives, you can always uplift each other's 'days by having a pleasant interaction.

5. Learn a new language. Take a class or join a group that can help you pick up a new language. Choose a language that's frequently spoken around you, so you can

connect with more people. You can also choose a language of a country that you plan to visit.

6. Join a club. Look online to find groups meeting in your area. You can find groups for everything. Whether you like sewing, reading, painting, or protesting, you can find a group doing just that. This will help you connect with others that you have something in common with.

By embracing what's around you, you can use your environment to help you thrive. Living your best life means putting yourself out there in new ways. Do the things you love and learn the things you've always wanted to learn. Shed self-doubt so that you can have frequent moments of fearless connection with others and your world.

Be Authentic

It is not always easy to be authentic. Being authentic requires that you reveal your true thoughts, dreams, and ideas. Gone are the days of people-pleasing. You can speak up for yourself, pursue the things you want, and talk with new people all while being totally authentic and kind.

Be nice to yourself and kind to others. Being your authentic self means that you're showing the world who you really are by being conscious of your actions and taking chances to demonstrate your values and loves.

Follow these tips for embracing authenticity:

1. Continue to love yourself. Increase your self-compassion practice by improving the way you speak to yourself throughout the day. When you're able to accept yourself in your head, that will show on the outside. You will feel confident and worthy. Your thoughts matter.

2. Make intentional time to get to know your community. Whether it's once per week or once every few months, get out and get involved. As you continue to follow through on this commitment, it will get easier, and it

29

will definitely be more fun than fear!

3. Practice gratitude. Gratitude is an excellent key to authenticity because it helps you get to a place where you feel grateful for your life and everything in it, good or bad. When you're having these feelings of gratitude, you're more likely to feel at peace with yourself.

4. Do what brings you fulfillment. Instead of doing or saying what everyone wants you to, take a pause and think about what is most fulfilling for you. That is what authenticity is about. It is just about you being you, exactly as you are. Love yourself for that.

5. Allow yourself to be inspired. Take a deep breath of fresh air, stretch your arms above your head, and listen to the sounds you love. When you're feeling inspired, your confidence goes up and you're more comfortable with yourself.

6. Increase interactions with those around you. By putting yourself in small, positive social situations, you can have even more practice with being truly you. Practice on the small

stuff, like ordering the food you want to eat for dinner or picking out the movie for your group of friends.

You can build authenticity over time. At first, it can be a tricky concept to work with because sometimes it can be difficult to catch ourselves being inauthentic. If you notice that you're people-pleasing or avoiding your truth, compassionately remind yourself that you have permission to be exactly who you are (and exactly who you are is enough).

Start by noticing the times when you're inauthentic and thinking about what you could do or say differently in future instances. For example, if you chose music that you don't like because you knew your friend would like it, you can decide that next time you will play the music you want to listen to.

Doing this on small things will build confidence to speak up when it really counts.

Let Go of Expectations

When you go out to a large concert or even a small dinner, do you find that you begin to play everything that you think might happen while you're out? Do you imagine negative conversations, rejection, or a negative memory being formed?

When you're excited about something, do you find yourself imagining how perfect it will be? Do you ever find yourself disappointed when things don't live up to your expectations? This is totally normal.

As humans, we crave certainty. It sometimes seems easier to assume that the worst will happen than to accept that we have no idea what will happen. There is something a bit insecure about letting go of expectations. It can feel like a lack of structure or security.

Let go of perfection

First, let's talk about the disappointment that comes when things don't meet our expectations. Imagine you're attending a party and expect to have so much fun, taking photos, laughing, and having the best night of your life. Your expectations set up your excitement for the entire night.

If you have expectations that things will be perfect, you will crash to disappointment as soon as things stop being perfect, even if they are still going well. Sometimes expectations are crushed even after a night that has gone wonderfully. Because it was not the perfect, exciting night you imagined, you feel a loss.

When you find your mind drifting toward expectations of perfection, take these moments as a sign that it's time to pause and release these expectations. Instead, you can say, "I am excited for what this evening holds," with a sense of curiosity instead of pressure.

If you find yourself disappointed when things did not go according to plan, reflect on the event and find what *did* go well. Maybe things that you had not even considered in your planning went well. Maybe it was just one thing that made the whole night seem terrible.

Let go of the worst-case scenario

It's easy to assume that the worst is going to happen.

For example, when you need to give an important speech, you might find yourself assuming that you're going to be a total failure. You may be putting unnecessary pressure on yourself to be outstanding, and you may find yourself assuming that you cannot live up to the greatness that you want to live up to.

If you're going on a first date, you might assume that your date will be horrible and that they will not like you.

How could you possibly know? By walking into situations with these negative attitudes, you're more likely to feel stress and fear while you're in that moment.

If you feel like the worst is going to happen, pause for a moment to remind yourself that you cannot tell the future. Remind yourself that you get to control yourself and your behaviors, no matter the situation. So, you can choose to walk into a new situation with a patient curiosity and an open mind.

Negative mindsets often take years to develop. It may be a habit that you picked up in an attempt to protect yourself from previous fears. You can find the beliefs that are not productive for you and choose to release them.

So, if you're assuming that people don't like you, or that things are not going to go your way, you can dive into that and learn more.

Focus on the moment

Letting go of expectations will enable you to live your best life because it's another layer of weight that you're removing from the things that keep you from being truly you.

Instead of having any expectations at all, positive or negative, learn to embrace the present moment for exactly what it is. You don't have to obsess over the past or try to predict the future. You don't have to try to read people's minds or try to predict their behavior.

Instead, take a pause and bring yourself to the present moment. This present moment acknowledgement comes as a result of mindfulness and can be applied to every area of your life, every day.

"Be mindful. Be grateful.
Be positive. Be true.
Be kind."

- *ROY T. BENNETT*

PRACTICE MINDFULNESS

Mindfulness is simply awareness of the present moment.

It's common to think frequently about the past and the future. You replay your day, remember childhood disappointment, and grapple with loss. You try to predict the future, assume the worst, expect perfection, or get disappointed before the next thing has even happened.

How often do you stop thinking about the past or the future, and instead consciously focus your attention on the here and now?

Mindfulness means you're giving your full mind to the present moment. There are many ways to practice mindfulness, and we will go over many of them here.

Mindfulness will have a powerful effect on your mind and your life. You will find that you have stronger emotion regulation, feel more at peace throughout the day, and enjoy yourself more than ever before.

Your self-compassion practice will be drastically improved when you begin to put mindfulness in your routine. Practicing mindfulness is helpful with self-compassion because it helps center you in reality and feel calm and accepting of everything around you, including yourself.

Living your fullest life means taking each moment as comes. You can appreciate every moment and look for each lesson.

Mindfulness

Mindfulness nonjudgmentally invites you the present moment. When you can sit in the present moment and have compassion and open-mindedness, you will be able to connect to yourself on a truly self-compassionate level.

When you're truly mindful, you will find a new peace of mind that brings about calm throughout your life and your heart.

Mindfulness is simply turning your attention toward the present moment. You can do this by implementing some practices to help you bring your mind to a present state.

It's a good idea to make time each day to practice mindfulness. You can begin by working on doing your typical routines in a more mindful way.

For example, you can mindfully brush your teeth by taking your time instead of rushing through.

Begin by getting your toothbrush wet and putting toothpaste on it. Notice your tube of toothpaste and the color of your toothbrush. You can do all of this without judging any of it as "good" or "bad." Begin brushing your teeth. Pay attention to the bristles on the brush. Notice the taste of the toothpaste and feel your teeth getting cleaner.

Pay attention to any tension you're holding. Relax your shoulders and jaw. Loosen your grip on your toothbrush a little bit.

If you begin your day like this each morning, you'll begin to notice a change. This is an excellent way to start your day and a great way to implement mindfulness.

You can find many ways to practice mindfulness. There are many avenues toward compassion and awareness of the present moment. Try many activities to find ways that work for you to practice mindfulness.

Consider these simple mindfulness activities:

1. Body Scan. You can release tension and come back to the center of the present moment by checking your body for tightness. Do this by sitting comfortably or laying on your back. Begin at your toes and work your way up your body, relaxing each of your muscles as you go.

2. Pay attention to your five senses. Name things you hear, see, feel, taste, or smell. By doing this, you're remaining observant of where you are right now, and you're

connecting yourself to this moment.

3. Practice mindfulness meditation. You can simply sit and pay attention to your breathing. You don't have to breathe in a particular way. Simply notice your breath.

   - Avoid judging intruding thoughts. Acknowledge them and then return your attention to your breathing.

4. Mindfully eat your favorite food. Sit with your plate in front of you. Look at all of the food and smell the delicious smells. When you take a bite, pay close attention to the taste and texture of each food.

5. Color in a coloring book. Coloring is an excellent mindfulness skill. It's fun and it's a great way to get your energy out without acting on it in a negative way. Pay attention to the colors and all of the shapes you're coloring. You can set a timer for 15 minutes of coloring and see how relaxed you feel at the end.

With all mindfulness activities, your thoughts will likely drift. If they do, simply come back to the moment. You never need to judge yourself for getting lost in thought again.

When you're truly mindful, you have no judgments on anything. You're able to simply sit in the moment and tolerate what you're going through. Mindfulness brings more enjoyment to each moment.

When you can truly appreciate this, you will find compassion blossoming. Having compassion in the present moment connects mindfulness to self-compassion. Self-compassion and mindfulness work together to create a full love for self and life.

Mindfulness and Self-Compassion

When you're able to truly be in the moment, you will have easy access to a deep well of self-compassion and compassion for everyone. When you're sitting in the present moment, pay attention to having compassion for the moment. Take that compassion and turn it inward.

Self-compassion comes from the moment, when you're able to truly give yourself the love and appreciation you need. When you're practicing self-compassion, you're embracing each part of you in every moment.

When you're mindful in the moment, take your attention to yourself. If judgments or regrets come up, simply respond with deep self-compassion. What would you say to your very best friend?

If you're suffering, how do you speak to yourself? If you made a mistake or lost an opportunity, how would you speak to yourself? In times when you're being critical of yourself, you can use mindfulness skills to increase your self-compassion and be better able to tolerate the present moment.

One effective way to arrive back at self-compassion is by taking a self-compassion break.

To begin, take a few deep breaths. Relax your shoulders and ease the tension in your jaw. Give yourself a hug and comfort yourself. Give yourself all of the kindness that you would give to your closest friend. Allow yourself to feel loved and grounded in the present moment.

Constantly Compassionate

When you've found self-compassion for yourself, you can begin to spread that compassion to all beings. Imagine your compassion growing and growing. By starting small with mindfulness, you will see all of the ways you can implement it in your life. Over time, you can continue to advance your practice and find even more appreciation for the present moment.

As your self-compassion grows, so will your compassion for all beings. Imagine your compassion growing and growing, until it encompasses the earth with love. You can feel that peace and calm by having a regular and consistent mindfulness practice.

Giving yourself compassionate attention can transform your life.

"Letting go means to come to the realization that some people are a part of your history, but not a part of your destiny."

- STEVE MARABOLI

LET LET GO OF WHAT HOLDS YOU BACK

Moving forward means letting go of the past. We can be grateful for what we've learned and gained from the past. However, staying in it and wishing to change it, or remaining resentful for many years, will stunt your personal growth.

There are many things you can move on from. In order to best glide forward and reach new heights of happiness and success, there are people to forgive, fears to move on from, and negative people to let go of. You can even let go of yourself and forgive yourself. Set yourself free from all of these things.

Let Go of Resentment

Resentment is one of the heaviest things you can carry with you. It limits genuine freedom. People can be unjust and hurtful. You never have to be okay with what anyone has done. When someone has done something to hurt you or someone you love, you're allowed to be angry.

The fact is, what happened is what happened. That is the first step to forgiveness. Practice radical acceptance. Begin by acknowledging that the reality is indeed the reality. Acknowledge it mindfully, without judgment.

All you need to say is, "yes, this happened." This is acceptance. Acceptance does not mean that you're okay with what happened. Acceptance will enable you to move forward from resentment.

Once you've come to acceptance, you can begin the process of forgiveness. Despite how you may feel, forgiveness does not require the person you're upset with to do anything. Forgiveness is all about you.

As with all things, forgiving becomes easier with practice

First, write down your resentments in a list. Begin with the people who are easiest to forgive, and work from there. When a person comes up who you want to forgive, you can take a deep breath and say, "I forgive you." While you're doing this, release tension in your body and allow yourself to relax and feel the resentment leaving.

You will need to do this process for some people multiple times.

Forgiveness is powerfully beneficial and will make your life more joyful and rewarding.

This is also a great opportunity to learn more about yourself. Use your feelings of resentment and your process of forgiveness to get to know yourself better. How can this inform your values? Where do you want to go from here?

Let Go of Fear

Most fears are imaginary. They are stories we tell ourselves about who we are and what is going to happen.

When you feel fearful of the future, you keep yourself from achieving your fullest truth. You have learned fear. At some point, fear has served you. Of course, there are rational fears. The fears to let go of are the ones you think of when you think of what fears are holding you back from being truly you.

When you imagine your fullest self, what fears have you shed? What fears are long forgotten? It's helpful to visualize yourself feeling this freedom. These feelings will motivate you to make your fullest life a reality.

When you find yourself feeling fearful, observe and name that fear. Use your rational mind to understand what fears are coming from your ego.

Observe the moments when you feel fearful. Then, watch what you do in response to that fear. Begin working on remaining open during these times of fear. Instead of closing off and going back into your shell, see what it's like to remain open even in the face of fear.

You have much courage within you. When you feel fear creep in, name it, sit with it, and release it. Being mindful in these moments is essential. Bring yourself to the present moment. Breathe in your courage, exhale your fear. Imagine the fear leaving your body and leaving you only with greater courage.

Let Go of Negative People

Are the relationships in your life serving you well? It's easy to get lost in a destructive relationship. Sometimes it's easier to stay friends with someone than it would be to stop being friends with them.

Remember, there are many people around you who relate to and appreciate you. The only way to find them is by loving yourself fully and putting yourself into the world around you.

The way you let people treat you says a lot about how you treat yourself. If you begin being kinder to yourself, you may find that you're better able to ask for what you need from those around you.

When you can ask for what you need from others, you're showing yourself respect and love. When you demand respect from others by demonstrating it to yourself, you will find your relationships beginning to improve.

You will know that a relationship is no longer serving you when you leave interactions with that person feeling worse than you did when you arrived. If this happens regularly, or you see a pattern of inconsistent behavior, or even if it's simply a difference in values, you might want to consider letting go of that relationship.

It can be intimidating to cut ties with a friend. However, it's a necessary part of growth. Sometimes you only need to be in someone's life for a short time so that you can both learn what you need to. You don't need to be friends with all of your friends forever.

One way to create structure around the kind of people you allow in your life is by setting boundaries. If you have a toxic friendship in your life, you can put boundaries in place to keep your needs clear.

For example, if you have a friend who is frequently intoxicated when you're together, and that upsets you, you can set a boundary that you will not spend time with that friend when they are intoxicated. This boundary is clear and not up for interpretation.

Setting boundaries like these can help keep your toxic relationships at bay, and new positive relationships will come forward.

How to Set Boundaries

Try these techniques:

1. Get quiet and think about your needs. You can write on a piece of paper about what you need in your life and what people are no longer helping you attain your greatest good. Let yourself write without judgment and see what feelings or needs come to the surface.

2. Establish your limits. Know where the line is for how much you're willing to tolerate.

3. Know what you need. In times of stress or frustration with a person, what are things that you need in those moments, based on how you feel? Do you need to leave? Do you need to end the interaction?

4. Communicate your boundaries clearly. Boundaries are a great guidepost because they are sturdy and you can simply repeat that boundary in response to any reaction you get back.

5. Be consistent in following through on your boundaries. Pay attention to how you feel when you do or don't follow through. If it's difficult for you to take a stand, keep practicing and see what happens.

6. Give yourself the okay to let go of these people that are causing harm or limiting you.

Allow Yourself to Let Go

Now, give yourself permission to do all of the healing and letting go that you need to. In order to most powerfully grow forward, you must commit to trusting the process fully. You can now let go of your past. You can let go of your regret, anger, fear. You can let go of the people that hold you back or don't believe in who your best self is.

When you're letting go of people, you can take that time to participate in your community in ways that will help you get closer to people who are better suited for this season in your life.

"When you truly love or want what you are pursuing, holding on can never be harder than giving up."

- MOKOKOMA MOKHONOANA

HOLD ON TO WHAT MOVES YOU FORWARD

When you let go of one thing, you're free to hold onto another. As you let go of the things that hold you back, you're now able to grab hold of the things that will propel you forward.

There are many things you can use to help move you forward. Start with the things that inspire you most and work from there.

In this chapter, we'll cover some great things you can begin to hold that will help you continue to grow. What is meaningful in your life and how can you pursue it? How can you use spirituality to ground you and move you forward? How can you best embrace positive experiences and give yourself what you need in your daily routines?

Clarify Your Values

Take a moment to think about the most important things to you. Think of your family, friends, work, and yourself. What words come up when you think about these things? What words come up when you think about what kind of person you want to be? These things are what you value.

You can narrow down your values to just a few core values that can help guide you in the right direction toward a fulfilling life. You can determine your values however you want to. What character traits would you most like to act on? Honesty? Humor? Integrity? Leadership? Family?

Think large, and then get smaller. Come up with a large list of values and then narrow it down. Think of about 4 - 5 values that you want to live up to on a daily basis.

Once you have those values selected, begin thinking about what it might look like if you put these values to action. For example, what would you do more of if you followed your value of humor? What would you do less of if you lived up to your value of family?

Imagine yourself acting out these values and keep them in mind as you go about your days.

Use these values when you're trying to make a decision about what the next right thing is. Use them to determine what sort of people you want to invite into your life. You can even use your values to give you confidence and meaning.

When you have a solid set of values, so many things will fall into place. Values make things straightforward and clear.

You will typically be able to tell if you're not living up to your values. Just as in mindfulness, when you find yourself straying from your values, nonjudgmentally come back to them.

Having your values solidified will help guide you through the rest of your life. You can start to set goals that will help you grow at exponential rates.

Goal Setting

Set goals that are realistic for you and that are based on your values. You can use your values to help you determine where you want to end up. When you bring your dreams into the mix, goals start to appear.

Set long term goals first. Think of your wildest dreams and then work from there to come up with some short-term goals that will help you in your day-to-day life.

Goals will help guide you to your true potential. You'll be better able to see the big picture when you know what you're really working for. When you don't have a big idea in mind, it can be easy to lose perspective.

By keeping your long-term dreams in mind, you'll be able to take a step back and see your purpose any time that you're feeling lost. Goals are the breadcrumbs that lead to the dream.

Explore Spirituality

If you can get to a place of peace and calm with the meaning of your existence, you will feel much more at peace in the rest of your life. No matter what your spirituality entails, you can choose how you want to tether yourself to your existence.

What brings you peace in the storm? What can you learn from each moment of your life? Imagine the things that bring you the most comfort. When do you feel the most connected to the world around you?

These methods will help you explore your spirituality:

1. Go somewhere peaceful and sit quietly or write. Think about a time or two when you've felt the most connected to the world around you. Think about a time when you've felt truly connected to your feelings of meaning in your life.

61

2. Look at the core of those moments. What were you feeling? What were you doing? What were you trusting?

3. Now, go do more of those things. If you enjoy sitting outside, go sit outside. Doing things that help you connect to nature is an excellent way to get to a spiritual place.

4. Volunteer. When you help others, you will feel a sense of calm that is rarely found elsewhere. This type of authentic human connection can improve your relationship with your ideas of spirituality.

5. Practice mindfulness. Practicing mindfulness daily is a great way to get more in touch with your spirituality. Sitting in that stillness can bring about transcendental experiences that can help you grow in new ways.

6. Talk with others about spirituality. If there are people in your life whom you admire, you can discuss their spirituality with them. Ask them how their spirituality informs the rest of their life.

You can use your feeling of spiritual purpose to ignite and bring calming inspiration to all areas of your life.

Having a larger idea of why you're here will help center you in the present moment and give you a stronger sense of security when you're full of existential angst. Holding onto spiritual habits that work for you will bring a new sense of strength to your life and your heart.

Embrace Your Greatness

Praise yourself each day and embrace the greatness that you truly are. When you truly begin to realize that you're completely worthy of love, you will also realize that you're unstoppable.

Feel your sense of greatness well up within you. During moments of mindfulness practice, feel your back straighten and your shoulders relax. Feel the inspiration flowing in your veins and enjoy the person you are.

Start by treating yourself when you need to. What are your favorite things to do? Start making time each day or each week to do the things that you love most. You deserve to have fun, and you can give yourself that fun by taking charge and believing in your worthiness.

Make kindness a regular part of your daily self-talk. You can do many things to remain in a place of compassion with yourself. For example, write yourself short and encouraging notes in the morning. You can use these to motivate you through the rest of the day. Who says you cannot tell yourself that you're proud of yourself?

Give yourself praise each day. You're allowed to praise yourself for getting out of bed, putting on shoes, or getting a promotion. Be proud of yourself for everything. You've worked hard to get where you are. By giving yourself praise, you're acknowledging your strengths and giving validation to yourself.

"For us to feel good emotionally, we have to look after ourselves."

- SAM OWEN

Self-compassion is a lifelong project and a daily practice. By loving yourself fully, the real you will come to the surface and you'll have a stronger understanding of the beauty within your life. By seeing this beauty, you'll be better able to live your most fulfilling life.

Shed the doubt that you hold onto. What self-doubt do you carry around with you? How does it affect your behavior? When you're able to see the areas in which you doubt yourself, you can begin changing self-sabotaging behavior that keeps you from your best self.

If there are relationships that are struggling in your life, you can either let them go or try to improve them. Doing nothing will not make anything better. You can improve your relationships with friends, community members, colleagues, and family by being patient and compassionate.

Showing compassion for others will help you practice it for yourself, just as being compassionate to yourself makes it easier to show compassion to others.

If you consider yourself an overthinker, you can bring your mind to a state of peace by shedding the various ways in which you over think.

Let go of the past. Let go of the things you've done that you feel guilty for.

Let go of regret. You can let go of regret by giving yourself permission to move forward. Write about the things you regret in order to take a step back and learn from them. There is always a lesson to learn if you're willing to look for it.

Use moments of regret as an opportunity for connection to all those who have experienced what you're feeling.

Release that little nagging voice.

You're your biggest bully. You no longer need to say harsh things to yourself in times of confusion or doubt. Perhaps you've noticed a constant narrator that is sometimes (or frequently) negative and destructive. There's no need for you to listen to this voice, as it only keeps you from pursuing your greatest self.

Instead of listening to the negative things you say to yourself, replace those things with positive phrases and thoughts. Instead of believing that you're a failure, see yourself as a learner.

Social anxiety and fears are common and necessary to move through if you want to adventure through life with openness. However, letting go of these fears can be difficult. You can begin by asking a friend to help you through social situations that make you nervous.

Jump into the adventure of the community around you. Peruse your community with the eyes of an explorer. Dive in and see what is in store. Take a quiet moment to truly participate in the world around you.

You can engage with your community by talking with others and being kind to them. Building community starts small. Starting small helps you build confidence in approaching new people if that is something that makes you nervous.

You can get involved with the world around you by being a tourist in your own town, trying something new with a group of people, or having a conversation with the barista at your coffee shop.

When you're diving into your community, do so with authenticity. The more you love yourself, the more comfortable you will be with being authentic. Increase the interactions with the people around you so that you can continue to practice being your true self and connecting with people from that level.

Let go of expectations. These expectations don't serve you. Instead, bring your attention to the present moment, where all is well and you're full of gratitude.

Mindfulness is an essential part of uncovering your true self-compassion.

You can practice mindfulness by paying close attention to what you're doing in the present moment. Choose an activity that works for you and make it a regular part of your daily routines. Use mindfulness to grow your self-compassion practice by loving yourself in each moment.

Let go of the things that keep you from growing.

By letting go of the things that no longer serve you, you're freeing yourself to experience life on entirely different levels. Let go of resentment, fear, and negative people. When you let go of resentment, you're releasing a weight off your shoulders that you may not have noticed before because it has been there for so long.

When you let go of fear, you're better able to fully embrace the future with curiosity. You will be better able to approach the present moment with a built-in sense of gratitude. When you feel fear creep in, remain mindful and express compassion for that fear while you release it.

Let go of negative people by setting clear boundaries with them. Get your needs clear and establish your limits. Give yourself what you need by recognizing your specific needs in stressful situations where you may need to have strict boundaries. Communicate your boundaries clearly and continue to follow through on them.

Take hold of the things that propel you in a healthy direction.

By embracing your true self, you can let go of the patterns that are not helpful for you. When you let go of those things, you can hold onto more positive things.

Get clear with your values so that you can use them as a compass on your journey in a fulfilling life. Look to your values to help point you in the right direction when you're not sure where to go. Your values determine the kind of person you want to be and how you want your behavior to reflect that.

Set realistic goals that are based on your wildest dreams. Determine what small thing you can do each day to work toward those dreams. Set goals each day, week, or month in order to keep yourself moving forward.

Acknowledge your greatness.

When you're able to look in the mirror and feel truly proud of who you see, you will know this practice is working. You can appreciate yourself, and you should.

You're allowed to be proud of yourself and grateful for what a great person you are. Take this deep love for yourself and find security in it. As you're living at your fullest potential, you're able to move forward and grow to new levels of knowledge.

When you love yourself, you can live fully.

Self-Acceptance

INTRODUCTION

When you think of having good emotional health, terms like happiness, self-esteem, self-confidence, optimism, and mental toughness likely come to mind. You might not consider the ideas of self-acceptance and contentment.

But isn't contentment what we're all seeking?

Contentment is the place where we don't need anything. We're completely satisfied as we are, as our life is.

Think of how many things you do each day in an effort to feel more content:

- You say or do things to impress others.

- You say or do things to avoid being ridiculed by others.

- You work at a job you don't like so you can make more money to buy things you want or to impress others.

- You exercise and diet beyond what is reasonable in order to look a certain way.

The list is really endless. We spend a lot of our day trying to feel more content. However, these things aren't the path to *radical* contentment.

The real secret is self-acceptance.

"The truth is: Belonging starts with self-acceptance. Your level of belonging, in fact, can never be greater than your level of self-acceptance, because believing that you're enough is what gives you the courage to be authentic, vulnerable and imperfect."

– Brene Brown

WHAT IS SELF-ACCEPTANCE?

There are many ways to look at self-acceptance. Some of them are more constructive than others. It would be a mistake to think of self-acceptance as a blanket acceptance of your weaknesses, bad habits, and negative tendencies in the absence of any responsibility to continue to improve.

Self-acceptance isn't an excuse for laziness and complacency. You can be content and still advocate self-improvement.

It also doesn't mean that you accept your fate and determine that nothing can or should be done to change your life.

Self-acceptance is a reckoning with yourself. It's an acknowledgement of your shortcomings, character, strengths, habits, and tendencies. It's about facing the truth and accepting that reality. Once you know where you are, you can make a reasonable plan to move forward.

Self-acceptance ultimately leads to contentment because you are no longer fighting with yourself. Because let's face it, **you cannot be both your #1 fan *and* your #1 enemy.** It's self-defeating.

You need to free yourself from self-punishment in order to be healed. When you release yourself from the negative thoughts that hold you back – and *accept* where you're at – you are setting yourself on a truly radical journey toward contentment, peace, and happiness.

But that's easier said than done. In the next section, we'll explore the reasons why self-acceptance can be so challenging.

"For me, art really starts with acceptance, self trust. Wherever you come to with art, it's perfect. You don't have to come with anything. What you bring to something is the art. That's where it's found. It's found within you."

– Jeff Koons

WHY ACCEPTING YOURSELF IS SO CHALLENGING

We're hard on ourselves. Many of us are more understanding and forgiving of others than we are of ourselves. It doesn't make a lot of sense. If anyone is going to be on your side, it should be you!

There are several common signs that you're being too hard on yourself:

1. **You dwell on your mistakes.** This accomplishes nothing positive. It does accomplish several things that are negative. Avoid doing this.

   o We're all human and make mistakes. Dwelling on mistakes makes you feel less capable and miserable in general.

2. **You compare yourself to others.** There's always someone richer, better looking, more musically talented, "luckier," or has children that do better in school.

   - **Comparing yourself to others is dangerous.** You don't know the other person's background or available resources. They may have a huge advantage.

   - You're also more likely to compare yourself to exceptional people. Do you compare your looks to the middle-age man or woman at work that has three kids? Of course not! You compare yourself to the 21-year old intern that models on the side.

3. **You don't give your own ideas a fair chance.** How many great ideas have you

had, but ultimately dismissed?

4. **You spend too much time thinking about your past failures.** Oh, the past. You chickened out and didn't ask Mary to prom. Or you majored in liberal arts instead of engineering. Maybe you didn't get that dream job. There's always something.

     - **If you focus on negative experiences, you're failing to accept yourself and your current reality.**

5. **You can't take a compliment well.** There are good things about you. It's okay when others acknowledge those things. Your inability to accept a compliment from others is a sign that you don't accept yourself.

6. **You're unrealistic.** Being unrealistic might be seen as being kind to yourself, but it's not. If you truly don't have what it takes to become an NBA star, or a Rhodes Scholar,

or a CEO, you're not doing yourself any favors by holding onto unrealistic expectations. You're ultimately being hard on yourself.

It's not easy to accept yourself. We've been taught that the ideal person is financially successful, athletic, attractive, cool under pressure, hilarious, creative, and the life of the party. Most of us will never check all of those boxes.

There are many signs that you're not as accepting of yourself as you could be. Be on the lookout for these signs. You probably don't accept yourself as much as you think!

"Acceptance of one's life has nothing to do with resignation; it does not mean running away from the struggle. On the contrary, it means accepting it as it comes, with all the handicaps of heredity, of suffering, of psychological complexes and injustices."

– Paul Tournier

9 WAYS TO BEGIN ACCEPTING YOURSELF

Accepting yourself is a process. It's a habit. **The little things you do, or fail to do, each day determine your level of self-acceptance.** Developing these useful habits and dropping the negative habits is a huge step in the right direction. It's hard to accept yourself any other way.

Be accepting of yourself each and every day by making these actions habits:

1. **Let go of your mistakes and failures.** Take the necessary time to learn from your negative experiences. Once you've done that, there's nothing else to be gained by them. Let them go.

o Decide how you can avoid making the same error in the future. Then move on.

2. **Only compare yourself to yourself.** Comparing yourself to someone else is like comparing a tree to a loaf of bread. There's no comparison. However, you can compare yourself to your previous results.

   o If you're doing "better," you have every right to be excited.

   o If you're coming up short, be excited that you know you can easily rectify the situation.

3. **Separate yourself from your emotions.** Your emotions are separate from you. They are something that you're experiencing, just like someone stepping on your toe. Observe them as a feeling in your body, or as a piece of paper blowing down the street. **Just**

observe them.

- A piece of paper blowing by doesn't have any control over you. Your emotions don't have to control you either.

4. **Be aware of what makes you unique and embrace it.** It might be your flaming red hair, your incredible IQ, or your compassion for animals. Maybe you're in the bottom 5th percentile for height. You're not exactly the same as anyone else.

   - **It's your uniqueness that potentially provides the most value to you and the world.**

5. **Let go of the things you can't change or control.** You're not accepting of your life or your limitations if you worry about those things beyond your influence.

○ Ask yourself, "Is there anything I can do about this?" If not, there's no reason to dwell on it.

6. **Do something that you've always wanted to do.** Avoid denying your impulses. If you've always want to learn how to play the bagpipes or write a sappy screenplay, now is the time. When you deny your healthy impulses, you're not accepting yourself.

7. **Be more assertive.** Let people know what you think. Give your opinion. Allow your voice to be heard. Do the things you want to do. Assertiveness is a form of honesty - about you and your own desires.

8. **Recognize your thoughts and feelings.** Examine your self-talk. Stand in front of a full-length mirror and take a good look at yourself. Notice your thoughts throughout the day. Acknowledge how you judge yourself.

- Most people distract themselves with TV, the internet, food, their smartphone, or some other strategy. This is to avoid spending time with themselves. Turn off the distractions and notice what happens.

9. **Continue evolving.** Those with little self-acceptance tend to be stuck. They can't move toward anything positive. Be honest with yourself about what you like and dislike and allow your life to evolve.

Treat each day as a new opportunity to practice self-acceptance. **You must choose self-acceptance if you want to experience it firsthand.** It won't happen by accident. Develop self-acceptance habits and drop your tendency to judge yourself harshly. Free yourself from your emotions.

> *"I think happiness comes from self-acceptance. We all try different things, and we find some comfortable sense of who we are. We look at our parents and learn and grow and move on. We change."*
>
> *– Jamie Lee Curtis*

SELF-ESTEEM AND SELF-CONFIDENCE

You can be aware of your shortcomings and still be happy with yourself. Your self-confidence doesn't have to suffer either. You can honest with yourself and still be a powerful force in the world.

You might be thinking, "I thought I was supposed to be honest with myself, not build myself up."

This is being honest with yourself. If you had a truly accurate picture of yourself and your situation, you'd be a lot happier with yourself and a lot more excited about life in general!

Build self-esteem and self-confidence simultaneously with these strategies:

1. **List your greatest successes.** Remember when you were at your best. Remind yourself how that felt.

2. **Make a list of the things you appreciate about yourself.** List three things each evening. See just how great you really are.

3. **Dress up.** You walk a little taller when you're wearing your nice clothes. You deserve to feel good. There's no reason to wait for a job interview, wedding, or funeral to look or feel your best.

4. **Live by your values.** When you live by your code, you feel good about yourself. You feel badly when you do the opposite.

5. **Set a small goal and achieve it.** Give yourself an easy path to feeling good and enhancing your life. Set an easy goal and taste success.

6. **Be kinder toward others.** If you're hard on others, you're probably hard on yourself, too. **Avoid saying anything negative and be a good listener.** That will get you 90% of the way there.

If you have sufficient self-esteem and self-confidence, self-acceptance is easier to find. **You're already pretty great,** so there's no reason not to recognize it. Treat yourself with the admiration and respect that you deserve.

MEDITATION AS A TOOL FOR SELF-ACCEPTANCE

Meditation and mindfulness are all the rage these days. Though they have been around for several thousands of years, they have enjoyed a new level of popularity. Even the scientific world is getting involved. A quick search on your favorite search engine will demonstrate just how interested the world is in these topics.

While meditation accomplishes many things, we're interested in self-acceptance. **Meditation is a powerful method of stripping away the extraneous garbage that stands in the way of realizing the truth.**

Meditation allows you to see your erroneous thoughts and beliefs more easily. It also provides more emotional control. When your emotions are appropriate, and proportionate, it's easier to accept yourself and others.

"When you are discontent, you always want more, more, more. Your desire can never be satisfied. But when you practice contentment, you can say to yourself, 'Oh yes - I already have everything that I really need."

– Dalai Lama

Follow these tips to incorporate a daily meditation practice into your life:

1. **Create a daily schedule you can keep.** It's much better to meditate each day for a few minutes than to meditate for longer periods of time a couple of times a week. Be realistic. Ideally, you can set aside at least 20 minutes a day.

   - Avoid the mistake of failing to schedule your meditation time. If you wait until you have time, you'll never do it.

2. **Find a comfortable spot.** You don't need much. **Any quiet spot where you won't be disturbed will work just fine.** A firm chair or a seated position on the floor will work. Lying down can even work, provided you can stay awake!

3. **Start small.** It's more challenging to sit with yourself for 20 minutes than you think. **Five to ten minutes is a good start.**

4. **Meditation is a relationship with yourself.** So, be nice to yourself. It's about self-acceptance and compassion for yourself.

5. **Focus on your breathing.** Feel the air moving in and out of your body. Feel the sensation of the air moving past the edges of your nostrils.

6. **Continue until your mind wanders.** You probably won't even catch yourself the first several times your mind drifts away. All of sudden, you'll realize that you've been thinking about work, school, dinner, or your neighbor's annoying dog.

7. **When your mind wanders, let those thoughts go.** Think of thoughts as clouds blowing by. You don't have to pay attention to them or be affected by them. Just allow them to pass through your attention and return your attention to your breath.

- Your mind will wander a lot at first. You might not even be able to last 30 seconds before you mind is off to another place. That's okay. Just keep going. **You'll get much better with practice.**

Meditation will show you that your mind creates thoughts. These thoughts lead to feelings and beliefs.

You'll also learn that you don't have to be affected by them. Being upset by your thoughts is a little like punching yourself in the face. Unclench that fist by allowing your thoughts to pass on through.

Most people spend so much time "thinking" and being influenced by their thoughts, they have a weak grasp of reality. The world is going on around you, not inside your head. **You'll have a more honest perspective of yourself, the world, and those around you if you can quiet your mind.**

You'll quickly learn to avoid being bothered by your thoughts. They'll move along on their own, provided you don't engage with them.

This is crucial to contentment. When you're not being energized by your extraneous thoughts, you'll experience real peace. When something negative happens, the event isn't the real issue, it's all the thoughts that run through your head.

Learn to deal effectively with your thoughts, and you can easily push past any self-doubts that keep you from accepting yourself and finding contentment.

"Health is the greatest possession. Contentment is the greatest treasure. Confidence is the greatest friend. Non-being is the greatest joy."

– Lao Tzu

SUMMARY

We're all seeking contentment, perhaps even more than happiness. But we need to view happiness as a side-effect of contentment. The fact is, contentment is a prerequisite to feeling happy. Everyone is driven by the need for contentment.

Some of us seek contentment through achievement or wealth. Others seek it through altruism or creation. Both can be dead ends. Where does it stop? Does a billionaire ever feel content, or does he continuously feel the need to create greater wealth?

Nothing external can ever provide life-altering, radical contentment. Contentment must be found from the inside through kindness, compassion, and self-acceptance.

SELF-AWARENESS

Self-awareness is the most important aspect of personal development. It determines nearly everything else, including whether you're able to stay motivated and achieve your goals. As you peel away the layers, you'll discover wonderful things about yourself when you simply become more aware.

With self-awareness, you can change deeply held beliefs if they don't serve you well. The journey of self-discovery is never-ending and filled with surprises and adventures in your inner landscape.

When you become self-aware, you know your strengths, weaknesses, and personality type. But it's more than this. Fully knowing yourself includes being aware of your thoughts and watching them objectively as an observer, without emotion or attachment.

For example, you might tell yourself, "Now I'm experiencing anger." You can then go on to ask yourself why you're getting angry and where that anger is coming from. Certainly, your soul within you is not angry. So who is?

"To have greater self-awareness or understanding means to have a better grasp of reality." ~Dalai Lama

Discover Your True Self

Go deeper into yourself and peel away the layers until you can see who you truly are. This is the sort of analysis and probing that will help you answer the question that great minds have asked across the centuries: "Who am I?"

You may be an artist, but that's only the face you show to the world. Identification as an artist can create limitations, too. By defining who you are, you may categorize yourself and put yourself in a "box."

For example, a commonly held belief about artists is that they can't or don't make much money. Do you want to define yourself that narrowly?

As you explore yourself, you'll discover that you're capable of transforming yourself and creating your own world.

You'll be able to see yourself as you really are. You can either try to escape from this knowledge, or welcome it with open arms as an opportunity for self development.

If you welcome it, you could change the traits you dislike and build on those traits you do like. Frequently, we have behaviors left over from childhood that served us well then, but don't work well for us as adults.

"A human being has so many skins inside, covering the depths of the heart.
We know so many things, but we don't know ourselves! Why, thirty or forty skins or hides, as thick and hard as an ox's or bear's, cover the soul.
Go into your own ground and learn to know yourself there."
~ Meister Eckhart

TURN THE SPOTLIGHT WITHIN

The only person you can change is yourself. When you choose to transform yourself, you'll notice changes in your environment, including in the people who surround you. The world is your mirror and both the negative and the positive situations you encounter are created by you.

When you find yourself getting irritated by someone, examine yourself to see whether you harbor the same negative trait that they're manifesting. This requires delving deep. Usually, you'll find the answer is yes. You likely possess the same trait in some form or another.

Take Emily, for example: She might find herself attempting to converse with her six-year-old nephew. The boy is anti-social, always glowering and scowling at people. He never speaks to anyone. When Emily tries to interact with him, even to smile at him, he scowls even harder.

This prompted Emily to call him a "bad boy," which made the six-year-old even more aggressive. Fortunately, this happened in the presence of some of Emily's good friends who gently pointed out her folly.

Emily turned the spotlight within. Why was the Creator showing her this little boy? Did she also lack respect for others? She realized the answer was yes. The moment this thought crossed her mind, she stopped feeling irritated.

Emily believes that everything has a purpose and that the people and situations we face are meant to teach us something we've been previously unable or unwilling to learn. This understanding has helped her use events in her life to become more self-aware.

Of course, in order to make decisions, you'll also make judgments. They're a necessary part of life. Yes, the boy was being rude, but the most important part of this situation is what Emily was able to gather from it. Likewise, you can use situations in your life to become more aware of yourself.

"Everything that irritates us about others can lead us to an understanding of ourselves."
~ Carl Gustav Jung

WHAT TO LOOK FOR WHILE DEVELOPING SELF-AWARENESS

To be self-aware means you're conscious of the following:

Your goals

The events, thoughts, and beliefs that make you happy and sad

Your strengths and weaknesses

Your values and beliefs

Your philosophy in life

Your achievements, how you accomplished
them, and what you learned from them

Your failures, how they came about, and
how to prevent them from recurring

How you relate to others

How you see yourself and others

BE AWARE OF YOUR MOTIVATIONS

Whenever you do or say something, be conscious of the reason behind it. If you scold a child, ask yourself why. Do you want to assert your seniority or authority, or do you actually want the child to improve their behavior for their own best interest?

"I think self-awareness is probably the most important thing towards being a champion."
~ Billie Jean King

WHAT IS YOUR PERSONALITY TYPE?

If you're not sure whether you're an introvert or extrovert, try this simple short quiz online: http://www.nerdtests.com/mq/take.php?id=19

Put simply, the introvert is more prone to self reflection and prefers solitude. He's more interested in his inner landscape. In contrast, the extrovert thrives on social interactions and is highly expressive. He's interested in the external. Chances are that you, like most people, have a mixture of both personality types. You may express some aspects of your personality in an introverted way and others in an extroverted way.

For example, at work, you may be more of an extrovert, a team-oriented person. You like the energy generated by a group of people working towards the same goals. You may feel uncomfortable and insecure when you're required to work on your own.

On the other hand, during your personal time, you may lean more towards enjoying meditation, reflection, and quiet activities, as opposed to pursuing the adventures of a social butterfly.

Once you're aware of your tendencies, you may want to get out of your comfort zone once in a while to increase your flexibility. In turn, this will enable you to be more comfortable in a diversity of situations.

"The outward freedom that we shall attain will only be in exact proportion to the inward freedom to which we may have grown at a given moment. And if this is a correct view of freedom, our chief energy must be concentrated on achieving reform from within."
~ Mahatma Gandhi

HOW TO FLEX YOUR FLEXIBILITY MUSCLE

Step out of your comfort zone with the following exercise:

1. On a piece of paper, sign your name. Notice the feeling of comfort. This is familiar. Maybe signing is even automatic for you.

2. Now write your signature with the other hand. Notice the difference? You'll probably do it more consciously. You'll pay more attention to the process. Does your

signature look like the one you created with the hand with which you usually write?

3. Write your signature another six times using alternate hands. You'll probably begin to feel more comfortable when writing with your non-dominant hand. The signature will also begin to look better. If you keep at it every day, you'll eventually be able to write your signature well with either hand.

In other situations, too, practicing a certain way of being or doing things, such as working on a project on your own, will widen your horizon and your possibilities.

"Everyone thinks of changing the world, but no one thinks of changing himself."
- Leo Tolstoy

"WHAT THE BLEEP DO WE KNOW?"

This famous documentary made in 2004 marries quantum physics with spirituality. You see how you create your world with every thought. It's a view shared by many quantum physicists as well as spiritual teachers such as The Buddha.

The TV series cites the example of the Japanese Professor Emote's photographs that reveal the transformation of water molecules through exposure to spoken and typed words, music, videos and pictures.

A simple molecule of water becomes a thing of beauty after a priest prays over it. A water molecule from a jar with the word "Hitler" written on it appears ugly.

Imagine then, how our thoughts and words affect us! The human body is about 70% water. This opens up a whole new world of revelation!

According to quantum physics, everything is inter-connected. We are one with everything. We influence our environment.

In the documentary, the protagonist Amanda, played by Hollywood actress Marlee Matlin, begins to transform her frustrated self. She remembers that the human body is comprised of 70% water and thoughts, and that emotion and words affect the molecular structure of water. We watch her becoming a serene, self confident being.

"Men are disturbed not by events, but by the views which they take of them."
~ Epictetus

THE IMPORTANCE OF APPRECIATION

Now that you know that your thoughts influence water, remember to thank your Creator whenever you drink a glass of water. Your appreciation and gratitude will turn it into an elixir.

Appreciate the air you breathe, the food you eat, the people you live with, as well as those you don't see, such as farmers who provide you with sustenance. No man is an island!

Do you see how becoming more self-aware can help you create the life you desire? When you see how you're affecting the world around you, you can transform it to align with your desires by transforming yourself.

UNITY CONSCIOUSNESS

In realizing how all things are interconnected, you've entered into the concept of "Unity Consciousness." Being self-aware includes seeing how you're connected to the rest of the world.

How do you attain this feeling of oneness with all things? One way of doing this is by not differentiating between the Divine and sentient beings. What you do to any of them, you do to the Divine.

"We cannot live only for ourselves. A thousand fibers connect us with our fellow men; and among those fibers, as sympathetic threads, our actions run as causes, and they come back to us as effects."
~ Herman Melville

SELF-AWARENESS AND THE TAO

Taoists urge us to believe in the goodness of our inherent nature, the True Self and the interconnectedness of all things. In Tao te Ching (Power of the Way) the author Lao Tzu, great sage and founder of Taoism, writes: "The great Tao flows everywhere. It nourishes the ten thousand things. It holds nothing back."

In this book, he gives us "three treasures" to help us experience unity with all things:

1. Compassion. With compassion, you don't condemn others for their mistakes, for you recognize these mistakes in yourself.

2. Frugality. The frugal one avoids being wasteful and going to extremes. Living

frugally, you can enjoy abundance. Your life will be as simple as your needs.

3. Humility. Humility dissolves the ego and thus removes all possibility of disharmony and conflict. Watch for signs of humility in yourself. True humility revolves around knowing your strengths and weaknesses, and being willing to take responsibility for your actions.

"He who knows others is wise. He who knows himself is enlightened."
- Lao Tzu

ACKNOWLEDGE YOUR NEGATIVE TRAITS

Embarking on the never-ending journey of self-awareness requires courage. While it's easy for us to think of our good qualities, our negative traits are often pushed aside. You may even find justifications for your negative thoughts and behaviors. One way to cultivate awareness of them is to look deep into yourself and write down all of your characteristics, positive and negative.

Avoid chastising yourself for your negative traits. Instead, know that everyone is an amalgam of productive and destructive qualities. It's the desire to change what doesn't serve you which distinguishes the self-aware from the deluded.

"You will not be punished for your anger. You'll be punished by your anger."
~ Traditional Buddhist quote

PERCEPTION IS THE KEY

Going back to our story of Emily, today Emily has reached a higher level of understanding of the nature of good and bad. She's realized that there is no such thing as good or bad. Everything is an emanation of the Divine. A "bad" situation can become "good" if it's perceived that way.

When Emily found herself jobless, her spiritual teacher suggested she clean the main hall of the temple every day. That would be her new "divine job." Trusting her guru completely, she went to the temple every morning and after sweeping and mopping she would be invited to have lunch with her guru and the nuns.

It was a joyous time for Emily because she chose to make it so. No one who saw her could tell that she was jobless and frustrated. In about two months, she found another higher paying job.

"Your vision will become clear only when you look into your heart.
Who looks outside, dreams. Who looks inside, awakens."
~The Dalai Lama

USING SELF-AWARENESS TO BE YOUR BEST SELF

1. Consider your strengths. This is the fun part. Make a list of your strengths and think of how they're contributing to your happiness and that of others. Some examples may include creativity, initiative, determination, self-reliance and empathy.

   If you find it impossible to list your good qualities, ask a friend or family member to write down what they like about you. This will give you leads, but avoid asking them when they're in a bad mood or annoyed by something you've done!

2. List your achievements. Make a list of ten of your accomplishments in multiple areas of your life. For example, you might list some social achievements, work successes, and achievements in the realm of personal growth.

    1. Next to each example, write down the skills you used to realize them. For instance, if you went shopping on your own for the first time, what new competencies did you pick up in the process? Maybe you learned navigational skills or discovered that you have good taste in clothes.

    2. Now enjoy your list of accomplishments, skills and competencies. Consider how you can use these in the future. Do you have

more than ten accomplishments?
Note the others too.

3. Write down your preferences and habits.
    Maybe you find yourself preferring a certain
    armchair or place at the dinner table. You
    probably have a morning routine with which
    you're comfortable. Maybe you feel out of
    sorts if you sometimes have to change the
    routine.

    Sticking to your routine is a great way
    to beat stress or take the edge off
    having to make difficult decisions that
    take you into uncharted territory. Be
    aware of your patterns and let go of
    those that aren't constructive, but
    don't hesitate to cultivate those that
    benefit you.

"Knowledge is learning something every day.
Wisdom is letting go of something every day."
~ Zen Proverb

Resolving Conflict by Becoming More Self-Aware

The cause of conflict is always within us. When you find yourself in an uneasy situation, check whether your ego is in the way. Usually conflict is caused by the need to assert your wishes or the desire to be right. Once you become aware of this in yourself, you can begin to resolve it.

Or it could be that you feel stressed out because of the emotions simmering within you. You may not be aware of them at first. For instance, there could be worry, fear, jealousy, anger, resentment, or frustration, sometimes all at once. At such times, take a deep breath and observe what's happening in your mind. This simple practice will help you to think more clearly.

*"Everything is based on mind, is led by mind, is
fashioned by mind.
If you speak and act with a polluted mind, suffering
will follow you,
as the wheels of the oxcart follow the footsteps of
the ox.
Everything is based on mind, is led by mind, is
fashioned by mind.
If you speak and act with a pure mind, happiness
will follow you,
as a shadow clings to a form."
~ The Buddha*

KEEP A JOURNAL

Self-awareness entails observing your thoughts and actions. One of the best ways to do this is by writing in a journal every day. If you keep putting it off and allow a week to go by without making notes, you may not recall everything important.

Keeping notes will help you see the patterns and values you've been harboring all along. Once you can identify these patterns, you can begin to change them if they're not leading to positive outcomes.

"I am, indeed, a king, because I know how to rule myself." ~Pietro Aretino

WAYS TO DEVELOP SELF-AWARENESS

When you're self-aware, you learn from your mistakes as well as the mistakes of others.

Here are other ways to develop self-awareness:

1. Adhere to good values. If you have humility, you'll be able to see your mistakes and faults and correct them. You'll also be able to accept criticism. With honesty, you can be open about yourself.

Courage enables you to look within without fear and carry on when faced with difficult circumstances.

2. Read self-help books. Read all you can on the subject and put what you learn into practice.

   Join a community of like-minded seekers. This is an effective and enjoyable way to develop self-awareness. It's easier to polish yourself into a diamond among a community of like-minded people than to go it alone. You may find self-help communities you enjoy online or at your church.

"Your task is not to seek for love, but merely to seek and find all the barriers within yourself that you have built against it."
~ Jalal ad-Din Rumi

SUMMARY

Your self-awareness will create the life of your dreams. This may not be an easy journey, but it's sure to be interesting and enjoyable. And the rewards are unfathomable.

Banishing Self-Destructive Behaviors

"I have never been contained except I made the prison." ~ Mary Evans

Self-sabotage, while seemingly easy to define, can be made up of a complex set of actions. If you've ever found yourself interfering with the positive parts of your own life, you've experienced this intricate set of thoughts, feelings, and behaviors. But don't worry... you can unlearn these habits today!

This section elucidates self-sabotage and explains how you may be defeating yourself and keeping yourself from reaching your goals. In case you're still not sure whether you engage in these behaviors, the impact of self-sabotage on your life is also discussed.

But best of all, we'll detail easy steps to help you banish self-destructive behaviors for good! By using these strategies, you can live the more satisfied and successful life you so richly deserve.

SELF-SABOTAGE DEFINED

Self-sabotage involves engaging in behaviors that lead to results you don't want. Maybe you've heard the old expression, "shooting yourself in the foot." If so, then you understand the concept of self-defeating behaviors.

When you do something that ultimately hurts or thwarts you in some way, you engage in self-sabotage. By performing these destructive actions, you bringing negative experiences and situations into your life.

However, self-sabotage is complicated because there's usually some element of temporary relief, short-term payoff, or avoidance of something negative initially in the process.

Unfortunately, these brief episodes of positive feelings only serve to reinforce the idea that there are benefits from engaging in the problematic behavior.

To further muddle the picture, you'll eventually begin to feel the negative longer-term results of your questionable behavioral choices. So even though there's an early payoff, you'll ultimately get stung when you engage in self-defeating actions. Although self-sabotage is quite common, your efforts to avoid performing these types of troublesome behaviors will be worth your while.

The process of self-sabotage usually begins in your thoughts and feelings. Then, you make a choice based on those ideas and emotions.

Here's an example of self-sabotage:

You've been going to the gym for several months, but then you went on holiday, skipped going to the gym for a few weeks, and gained 15 pounds.

You're embarrassed and you don't want anyone to see you like this, so you choose to stop going to the gym entirely. That way, no one will see you've gained weight, and definitely nobody will see you in your now ill-fitting workout clothes.

The immediate consequence of your choice is that you don't have to risk being stared at by the others at the gym. You won't have to even momentarily experience the humiliation you feel about your weight, particularly in front of people you perceive as thin and dedicated to their health.

You feel a bit relieved. You think, "I'm so glad I don't have to deal with the whole health club thing." However, the ultimate result of your decision not to go to the gym is that you hold on to the extra 15 pounds or put on even more weight. Is this what you were hoping for?

Obviously, those results are opposite what you wanted when you joined the gym. The decision to skip exercising and avoid your feelings of discomfort only compounded your challenges in losing weight. This decision exemplifies self-sabotage; not only do you not get what you want, but you get more of what you don't want!

"Self-sabotage is when we say we want something and then go about making sure it doesn't happen."
~ Alyce P. Cornyn-Selby

HOW SELF-SABOTAGE IMPACTS YOUR LIFE

As you might surmise, self-sabotage can drastically affect your life. Self-defeating behaviors will most likely bring unfortunate circumstances your way.

Check out these important points about how self-sabotage reduces your quality of life and results in unplanned consequences:

- Self-sabotage becomes easier over time. When you choose to practice self-sabotage, your choices become easier to repeat. You may fall into a habit of doing whatever is necessary to avoid initial uncomfortable feelings, thoughts, and situations.

- Self-defeating behaviors cause unintended consequences. Unfortunately, there are long-term results of your choices and behaviors that you might not expect and therefore are unprepared for. Like in the example above, often the long-term effects are the exact opposite of what you originally wanted.

- Any positive results of self-sabotage are short-term. Remember that any seeming benefits you experience due to self-defeating decisions aren't long-lived. Some examples of short-term positive results are:

- You get out of giving a short speech to the supervisors at work so you won't feel anxious. Although this may seem like a great benefit, you lose your opportunity to practice speaking in front of others, which could reduce your anxiety next time. Instead, now you have reinforced the idea that you are too scared to speak to a group.

- You initially feel better about not being chosen to complete a big project at work: no stress! Plus, you won't have to do as much work as your co-workers at the moment. The long-term consequences of this can be diverse, but one of the biggest effects is that you have less opportunity to practice working under pressure. Therefore, you don't get better at it.

- You choose to stay with your abusive partner; therefore you don't have to pack up and find a place to live. Clearly, the long-term results of this choice can be dire, regardless of how much stress it may alleviate in the short-term.

- You won't have to sweat it out in an uncomfortable job interview since you didn't apply for the position. What? You're okay with only applying for jobs that you know you can get? You don't want to advance your career? The long-term results of this choice can lead to lower income over your lifetime, reduced self-esteem, and less job satisfaction.

- You keep hanging out with familiar people even though they aren't very positive. After all, it's easier than making new friends. This one can affect everything in your life. We become like the people we spend the most time around, so if you want to be happy with your life, affiliate with happy people!

- Regular self-sabotage drastically alters your life. The scariest aspect of self-sabotage is that if you make it a habit, in several years' time (or less!), you may find yourself not living the life you truly want. In fact, you'll likely experience great difficulty accomplishing the goals that you've set for yourself. Essentially, you'll stop believing in yourself.

Self-sabotage occurs over all periods of time, from minutes to years. Although you might experience a brief period of feeling better after an incident of self-defeating behavior, as time goes by, you're bound to experience unpleasant consequences.

"The haft of the arrow had been feathered with one of the eagle's own Lures. We often give our enemies the means of our own destruction."
~ Aesop

DO YOU SELF-SABOTAGE?

The nature of self-defeating behaviors is that they tend to be pervasive in the lives of people who engage in them.

If you self-sabotage sometimes, you probably self-sabotage much of the time. This becomes your primary way of thinking, choosing, and relating. Self-sabotage comes in many forms.

These examples show how you might be practicing self-sabotage:

- Drinking too much alcohol at social events. If you drink a bit more when you're going to be around new people, you may help yourself relax a bit and be a better conversationalist. However, don't be surprised if you occasionally make a fool of yourself instead.

- A function of drinking too much is a reduction in your good judgment. Isn't that the last thing you want if you're hoping to meet new people and make new friends?

- Saying "yes" when you'd like to say "no." Agreeing to do extra tasks when you have no real desire (or time) to do them is a classic way to self-sabotage.

- In fact, if you end up not getting something done when you agreed to do it, your friends and family will be disappointed, annoyed, or even angry with you. Most likely, these were not the results you were looking for when you said "yes" to the task!

- Insisting on your own way. Many of us do this out of a desire to seem knowledgeable and capable. But how do you suppose people feel about you if you refuse to cooperate and, instead, must have things your way? Do they respect you or see you as a person of knowledge and wisdom?

- If your goal is to be respected and taken seriously, you're self-sabotaging if you insist on having your own way all the time.

- Reacting instead of responding. Acting out your feelings isn't always best. Sometimes, you need to take a step back and evaluate the situation before you take action.

  - For example, perhaps you feel anxious so you avoid doing something, even though you know that you ought to follow through. Or perhaps you feel angry about something a colleague said. Self-defeating behavior in this case might include lashing out at them, which would just cause further friction in your relationship.

- Believing and behaving as if you're always right. Deep down, if you feel you "must" be

142

right and others must be wrong, you
probably lack true confidence. Otherwise you
wouldn't care what others thought.

- o When you behave this way, you
destroy your relationships with others.
And that's most likely very contrary to
your true goal.

- Refusing to take care of your body. How can
you work hard, enjoy the love of others, and
live a healthy, fulfilling life if you don't take
steps to take care of yourself? Regular
exercise is required for all. Ignoring that fact
is a refusal on your part to do all that you can
for yourself and your body, which is
indisputably self-defeating.

- Maintaining an unhealthy diet. Consistently
eating poorly isn't healthy, whether you're
skipping your fruits and vegetables or taking
in too many calories.

- o Probably the most common self-
defeating behavior in the U.S. is
knowingly overeating and consuming

high fat, low-nutrition foods. It's self-sabotage in its purest form.

- Avoiding things you don't want to do. Whether the object of your avoidance makes you anxious or you think it requires too much work, refusing to participate in some things can sabotage your efforts to have a fulfilling and successful life.

- Taking a passive stance to avoid a fight. Perhaps there are times when your feelings matter but instead, you just keep your thoughts and emotions to yourself so you don't rock the boat. Later, though, you end up in a swamp of difficulties because of initially holding in your honest responses.

- Procrastinating. Even though you tell yourself you want to do something, you just keep putting it off. Before you know it, you've missed the deadline or you're still in the same position you didn't want to be in.

  - The short-term payoff may be more time for other things initially, but the long-term results always include increased stress.

- Not finishing what you've started. Whether it's that painting you started that's been in your closet for years, the scrapbook from your last vacation, or the bookshelves you were making out in the garage, perhaps you have a habit of not finishing things. Eventually, you become frustrated from all your unfinished projects.

- Being indecisive. Perhaps you just let time go by without making a decision about something important in your life.

  o You believe you're escaping the stress of making the decision when, in fact, you're letting a wonderful opportunity go by. This is how people miss their opportunities to marry someone they love or get that new job they've been dreaming about.

- Avoiding getting a handle on your finances. You've convinced yourself your finances are out of your control. This way, you don't have to make any efforts to correct them. You simply blame it on your boss or the economy. This self-sabotage costs you money and a more secure lifestyle.

- Taking a pessimistic approach to life. When you consistently focus on the negative aspects of your existence, you vastly limit your choices in life. A negative perspective means you simply won't see certain options. You'll be stuck in a never-ending cycle of pessimism.

- Non-suicidal self-injury. In its most extreme form, self-sabotage can be physically unhealthy and even dangerous. Non-suicidal self-injury, NSSI, is a newer term for self-injurious behaviors, like cutting yourself, sticking pins in your skin, or burning yourself intentionally with matches or lighters.

  o Although those who engage in NSSI have reasons, such as stress or depression, these behaviors usually have the unintended consequences of embarrassment, avoidance of others, and social isolation.

The range of human self-destructive behaviors is wide and deep. There are a multitude of methods you might be engaging in, including self-defeating thinking, choices, and actions. Contemplate your own thoughts and decisions to determine if you're taking part in any self-sabotaging behaviors.

"This is how women self-sabotage and self-destruct. Unless we have constant witnesses to our hard work, we are convinced we pull off every day of our lives through smoke and mirrors."
~Sarah Breathnach

CHANGING YOUR LIFE STRATEGY: BANISHING SELF-SABOTAGE

Although letting go of your self-sabotaging behaviors isn't always easy, you can succeed if you make it a priority. Thankfully, there's a full range of strategies you can employ to help yourself avoid self-sabotaging behaviors.

To start your journey of eliminating self-destructive behaviors, commit to follow these steps:

1. Acknowledge that you engage in self-sabotage. Just like the first step in Alcoholics Anonymous, it's important to admit to yourself that you have a challenge before you can do anything to change it.

2. Write out how you self-sabotage. This exercise will feel like you're cleaning out the clutter of a closet, only it's your mind and emotions you're sorting through instead.

148

Keep thinking and writing until you've listed all the ways you engage in self-defeating behaviors.

3. Next, put down specific incidents where you recognize that your thoughts, choices, or behaviors were self-defeating. Go back for at least the last year or two. Claim full responsibility for your thoughts and actions. Now is the time to step up and do whatever is necessary to let go of the self-defeating thinking and behaving. Own it.

4. Plan your responses to challenging situations. Write them down! For each of your episodes of self-sabotage you wrote down in Step 2, record how you'll respond in a similar situation from today forward. Be specific. For example:

    1. "I will not avoid going out with friends just because someone I've never met will be there. Instead, I'll go with them and make an effort to talk to the new person. It's okay if I feel some anxiety! I won't allow my tense feelings to push me toward a decision that will ultimately prevent me from making

new friends, which is important to me."

5. Share your plans with a close friend or family member. Let someone know what you're working on. This part is important: ask them to confront you whenever they see you engaging in any self-sabotaging behavior. If you choose someone you trust, you'll believe them when they tell you you're self-sabotaging.

   If your friend comes to you to share that you're about to self-sabotage, carefully consider the information. Then thank them for telling you and ask them to continue to follow through with letting you know in the future about such behaviors.

6. Tell yourself you're worth the effort. Those who fall into repeated patterns of self-sabotage have low self-esteem and simply don't feel worthy of experiencing the lives they want. This is no secret.
   Repeat to yourself that you're worth the time and effort to change your self-defeating thinking and behavior.

7. Get out of the rut: start believing in yourself. Rather than put yourself down, give yourself some props for making it this far and for recognizing your self-defeating ways.

    Keep reminding yourself that you're letting go of the old style of living where you lacked confidence and determination. Make a decision to believe in yourself again.

8. Make a vow to yourself and a close friend. Commit to working to decrease and eventually stop engaging in self-sabotage. Say it out loud, to yourself and to your friend. If it helps you, feel free to say it to yourself in front of your bathroom mirror.

9. Use thought-stopping techniques to end unhelpful thinking. Negative thoughts can lead to self-sabotage. Whenever unproductive thinking begins, imagine a big red light in your mind, blocking out the negative ideas. Then, imagine a green light while choosing to replace the negative cognition with a positive one.

For example, let's say you're trying to eat healthier. As soon as you begin thinking about eating doughnuts, visualize a big red light. Then, think about eating an apple instead. Visualize a green light as you get the apple and bite into its crunchy sweetness.

10. Give yourself positive reinforcement. Making changes can be challenging. Using the example in Step 4, remind yourself during your evening with new friends that you made the right choice to get to know more people. Give yourself a mental pat on the back. You're going for your goals. Good for you!

11. Acknowledge your new, positive feelings and experiences. Staying with the example in Step 4, maybe you met three new people or made a real friend. Perhaps you laughed all evening and really had a great time. You might have even gained some confidence regarding socializing with new people.

12. As you begin to make different choices, you'll notice a pronounced drop in the number of your self-sabotaging actions. Bask in the positive emotions you feel about making healthier choices.

13. Educate yourself. Read a variety of self-improvement books about feelings to be better informed about what goes on inside of you. Engaging in self-study enriches your life in many ways and will help you re-focus your efforts on what you truly want.

    Here are some examples:

    Feeling Good: The New Mood Therapy by David Burns.

    The Book of Awakening: Having the Life You Want by Being Present to the Life You Have by Mark Nepo.

    Change Your Thoughts - Change Your Life: Living the Wisdom of the Tao by Dr. Wayne W. Dyer

Don't limit yourself to these, though!

There are abundant options in the self-help section of your local bookstore and more are written all the time.

If you find some that appeal to you more than the titles above, read them instead. This is all about self discovery, and that starts with tuning in to what you really want!

14. Keep your eyes open. Vigilantly monitor your thoughts and emotions. Notice when those self-destructive ideas creep into your mind. Stay in touch with your feelings. This way, you'll have greater awareness and can evaluate emotions and thoughts before they become behaviors.

15. Give yourself permission to think outside the box. Be willing to let new and foreign ideas into your head. Allow yourself to engage in new ways of thinking.

16. Consider professional help. If you don't feel like you're able to decrease your self-sabotaging behaviors, consider seeking professional assistance. Therapists, social workers, life coaches, and mental health counselors will help you confront your

unhealthy thoughts and behaviors and develop effective ways of dealing with them. Many people seek professional assistance at some point in their lives, and doing so can benefit just about anyone.

17. Persevere. Although there may be times when you feel overwhelmed by your ability to self-sabotage and contemplate giving up, if you persevere, your life will get better. Look back over these steps often. Re-read what you wrote about the ways you self-sabotage and how you'll overcome it.

As you practice these steps, you'll discover new ways to approach your challenges. You'll find that you possess greater strength and courage. One day, you'll look back and notice that you've come farther than you ever imagined possible. That day is worth all of the challenges between here and there.

Renew your commitment to yourself as often as needed. When making a commitment, all of us occasionally veer off-track. When you notice this, make a new commitment to yourself to continue in your endeavors to banish self-sabotage.

To do away with self-defeat for good, place these 17 steps on your refrigerator or by your bedside table where you'll see them every day. Review them often. Once or twice a day is a good place to start. Take time to think about what you're doing in your efforts to end your self-sabotage.

Keep your wish to banish self-destructive acts in the forefront of your mind. Your awareness is critical to your recovery.

"My definition of a mistake is when you don't follow your rules.
And if you don't have rules, then everything you do is a mistake.
And self-sabotage occurs when you keep repeating the same mistakes
over and over and over again."
~ Van K. Tharp

SUMMARY

Self-sabotage involves a complicated set of circumstances that ultimately short-circuits your ability to meet your goals.

Repeated episodes of self-defeating behaviors will have devastating effects. And the ways you might be self-sabotaging are diverse. Most of us engage in this in some form, and for many of us, it pervades our lives.

However, today we've begun the path toward banishing self-destructive behaviors. Free yourself from self-sabotage; Free yourself of self-doubt. Set forth to manifest our desires, to achieve your goals and live the life you've envisioned for yourself!
~pbts

Don't wait for the stars to align, reach up and rearrange them the way you want. Create your own constellation
~Pharrell Williams

www.ingramcontent.com/pod-product-compliance
Lightning Source LLC
Chambersburg PA
CBHW052356090426
42739CB00011B/2392